# RETAIL

# MASTERY

## The Handbook for Massage and Bodywork Practitioners

# RETAIL MASTERY

*First Edition*

**The Handbook for Massage and Bodywork Practitioners**

Cherie Sohnen-Moe
Lynda Solien-Wolfe

# Retail Mastery

## The Handbook for Massage and Bodywork Practitioners

Published by Sohnen-Moe Associates, Inc.
Phone: 520-743-3936 — FAX: 520-743-3656
email: sma.info@Sohnen-Moe.com
websites: www.Sohnen-Moe.com
www.facebook.com/SMA.biz
www.facebook.com/RetailMastery

ISBN: 978-1-882908-15-8
We have done our best to acknowledge all sources and contributors. If we have erred, let us know and we shall make corrections for the next printing.

Cover design: Deanna Sylvester
Cover image taken on location at
Rooted Therapeutic Massage
and Bodywork, Tucson, AZ
First Edition, 2017

Illustrations: Deanna Sylvester
Book/Interior Design: James Moe
www.RetailMastery.com
Printed in the United States of America
Last digit is print number: 9 8 7 6 5 4 3 2 1

For Cinder
and Princess
In loving memory

# Table of Contents

# Preface
## Drive Your BUS to Success

Cherie Sohnen-Moe and Lynda Solien-Wolfe have been collaborating for several years on the topic of retailing. They have facilitated workshops, written articles and blogs, and host a website and a Facebook page on this topic. They are both passionate about the importance of retailing in enhancing clients' wellness, as well as providing financial support for practitioners.

Lynda coined a phrase that has inspired them throughout this adventure: When it comes to retailing, you need to drive your BUS to selling success!

**B** Believe in the products you use

**U** Use the products in your sessions

**S** Supply samples to your clients

Sohnen-Moe Associates is offering readers of *Retail Mastery* direct access to the resources (**https://ya250.infusionsoft.com/app/page/ retail-mastery-resources**) mentioned throughout the book.

# About the Authors

**Cherie Sohnen-Moe** is an author, business coach, and international workshop leader. She has been a successful business owner since 1978. Before shifting her focus to education and coaching, she was in private practice for many years as a massage and holistic health practitioner. She has served as a faculty member at the Desert Institute of Healing Arts (DIHA) and the Arizona School of Acupuncture and Oriental Medicine (ASAOM).

Cherie has written hundreds of articles that have been published in over 15 national and international magazines. She is the author of the classic success book, Business Mastery. It is in its fifth edition, with more than 450,000 copies in print to date, and is recommended by more than 1,000 healing arts associations and schools worldwide (with approximately 400 schools requiring it in their curriculum). Cherie is also the author of *Present Yourself Powerfully* and *The Art of Teaching*. She is the co-author of the ground-breaking book titled *The Ethics of Touch*; this book is used in more than 700 schools and associations with 200+ requiring it in their curriculum. Cherie is also a contributing author of Teaching Massage: Fundamental Principles in Adult Education for Massage Program Instructors, and was interviewed for a chapter of *SAND TO SKY: Conversations with Teachers of Asian Medicine.*

Cherie holds a degree in psychology from UCLA and has extensive experience in the areas of business management, training, and creative problem solving—which combines well with her ability to support others to achieve what they want in life. Between her educational background and life experiences, the wisdom garnered from working with hundreds of clients and thousands of participants in her workshops and classes she has taught in schools, and the knowledge gained from researching hundreds of articles and several books, she is a strong resource.

She is active in many professional and community organizations. She is a founding member of the Alliance for Massage Therapy Education (AFMTE), has served on the board since 2010 and was president from 2015-2017. Among her honors she has received the Distinguished Service Award and the Professional Achievement Award from the American Society for Training and Development (ASTD), the Outstanding Instructor Award at the Desert Institute of Healing Arts, and is listed in several editions of Who's Who. Cherie is a 2012 Inductee to the Massage Therapy Hall of Fame.

She lives in Tucson, Arizona, with her husband, Jim.

**Lynda Solien-Wolfe** is a licensed Massage Therapist, esthetician, continuing education provider, writer, and business consultant. She is a strong supporter of massage therapy research, and an avid consumer of massage therapy. Lynda co-owns a day spa in Merritt Island, FL since 1994, where they have continually sold retail products since their opening. Lynda is the Vice President of Massage & Spa for Performance Health, the manufacturers of Biofreeze, Bon Vital, Thera Pearl, and Thera-Band wellness products. She has been with Performance Health since 1998 in a variety of positions.

Lynda has helped shape the massage therapy profession to have greater respect and acceptance. She has travelled to Asia, Europe, Australia, Canada, the Caribbean, and throughout the United States to spread her message and passion of the benefits of massage therapy. She has been very active in the massage and spa industry and has served in a variety of volunteer capacities, including the Florida State Massage Therapy Board. She has received many accolades for her dedication to the massage therapy profession, among them being a 2011 Inductee to the Massage Therapy Hall of Fame and receiving the William C. "Bill" Lindsey Layperson Chiropractic Award at the 2017 National Florida Chiropractic Association meeting.

Lynda is currently the chair of the Massage Makes Me Happy Initiative for the Global Wellness Institute and led the movement to create the Global Massage Makes Me Happy Day.

She calls the Space Coast of Florida home, with her son, Colton.

# Retail Mastery

The Handbook for Massage and
Bodywork Practitioners

# Introduction

Product sales are a great diversification method; the profits from the sales add an additional income stream that can defray overhead expenses. It is hazardous—physically, emotionally, and financially—to rely on your hands-on work as the sole source of your livelihood, particularly if your work requires intensity.

Product sales adds value to your sessions, extends the benefits to the client's home, and increases your bottom line. Product sales is a natural extension of the standard of care and healing already associated with wellness practitioners. You already have a relationship with your clients; retailing is simply another avenue of supporting your clients in their wellness.

Clients like to get products from you and appreciate the convenience of purchasing from you. They most likely get more education, service, and support with the products they buy from you than those they buy from a retail store or online. You save them time when they don't have to make a special trip to buy an item, spend hours researching online, or wait days or weeks for it to be delivered. Most clients would rather purchase products directly from you (their trusted practitioner) than from an impersonal company. They expect you to have more knowledge than they do about these products and trust your recommendations, especially those products that are used in the session itself. Plus, some are willing to pay a slight premium for the convenience. By selling clients the right products, you help them reduce their stress and improve their health beyond your treatment.

# 1
# Boost Your Bottom Line While Serving Clients

Most people who get massage and bodywork are looking for solutions to their health issues or wanting support in achieving their wellness goals. You have access to a wide variety of products (many of which aren't easily available to the general public) that can help clients with those needs and goals.

There are wonderful self-care products your average clients cannot find at their local health emporium; many of these products aren't directly available to retail consumers, they must be purchased by a practitioner and then sold to the client.

Suggesting someone purchase a product (e.g., a self-massage tool, a topical analgesic) for use between visits is on the same level as referring a client to another practitioner, providing educational handouts, or demonstrating self-care techniques.

We believe that you do your clients a disservice if you don't have products they can purchase. Many people are overworked and time management is a problem. If you can save them the time of buying a product elsewhere, then you've simplified their lives—and that's priceless. Clients with tight schedules may not have the time to fit in both a treatment and go to another location to purchase wellness products. You don't want them to have to choose one over the other. After all, they might not choose the treatment.

Consider how many times you used a product on a client and she said, "Wow that feels great! What is it?" and you responded by just stating the name of the product. Instead, you could tell the client the name of the product, mention that it's for sale in the waiting area, and give her a brief suggestion about its use, such as,

"This will really help if you apply a small amount before going to bed tonight. If you're interested, We can explain it more after the session."

We have received sessions where the practitioner used a really nice product or had great music playing, and didn't offer those items for sale. This was a missed sales opportunity for the practitioner—and disappointing.

Massage therapist Robert Flammia of Berkeley, California, sells a variety of gels, balms, books, and massage tools. He sees product sales as a way to increase his massage practice:

> Selling touch is perhaps one of the hardest things to do. Selling items that are physically or psychologically related to touch can be much easier.

Benny Vaughn—who has 40-plus years in practice and is known as the father of sports massage—doesn't differentiate between selling products and serving clients well. Vaughn says,

> In a thriving massage therapy practice, I see it not as retailing, but part of the therapeutic experience for the client. When I make it easy and convenient for a client to access products that can extend and enhance the massage therapy experience, then I am providing full customer service. [i]

Selling products can also be an excellent introduction to other services you offer. For instance, if you offer spa treatments (such as body scrubs), carrying a selection of scrubs for clients to buy might encourage them to try the product at home. They may then realize that they would like to receive a spa treatment from you.

## Your Unique Position

As a massage or bodywork practitioner, you already have a unique position with your clients, and retailing is simply another avenue of supporting your clients in their wellness. Some of the contributing elements to this unique position are the following:

- **Knowledge**: You have a broad knowledge base of techniques and products to help clients achieve their wellness goals.
- **Experience**: The longer you work with any given client, the more experience you have in what works and doesn't work for that client.
- **Built-in Trust**: As a practitioner, your client's wellbeing is literally in your hands. Because of the nature of the therapeutic relationship, you have already established a deep level of trust.
- **Time**: Most practitioners spend almost an hour (and often much more) with their clients every time they see them. Hopefully you see your clients on a regular basis. This is very unique: Unlike many other healthcare providers, most practitioners spend quality time with clients. This provides you with ample opportunities to build rapport, establish credibility, and ascertain your clients' needs and wants.
- **Power to Help and Recommend**: You have intimate knowledge of a client's needs, goals, wants, and conditions. Combining that with your product knowledge puts you in the position to truly help clients and make sound recommendations.
- **Help Clients and Earn Extra Income**: Since the majority of the products you sell are directly related to wellness, you are in a total Win-Win position.
- **Simplicity**: You don't need to be a retail store. You can stock a handful of key items.
- **Space**: You don't need a large storefront. You can even sell products when doing outcalls. You can purchase a Rolling Display Case that opens up with products neatly arranged for clients to see. You can even use the top of the case

to display additional items or hold your session supplies, brochures, and business cards.

What makes you stand out from the crowd is that you know your clients' needs and you can match the services and professional grade products that can help those clients.

## Extend Session Benefits

Clients see massage therapists for many reasons, ranging from stress reduction to injury rehabilitation to getting fit to pure pampering. Clients often benefit more from other things than the actual hands-on portion of the session. Some of the most profound outcomes result from those other things, such as: the client experiences someone (you) who truly listens without judgment, or the client experiences being the center of the universe for an hour. This also applies to products. You increase the benefits your clients receive by using appropriate products in the treatment, and offering those items for sale. After all, there is only so much that you can accomplish in a given session.

Extend the session benefits at home by providing clients with products that they can use between appointments. This can be from a direct therapeutic point of view, such as a self-massage tool or a book on stretching, to recreating a relaxation response. Ideally, you use some of these items in your sessions so your clients associate those items with their experience of your work.

Here is an example of using a product in your session that clients can purchase for home use: A client comes in for a treatment and at the end you apply kinesiology tape to an area that is easily accessible to the client. You demonstrate how to apply the tape and tell the client she can purchase a roll to apply the tape herself between sessions.

Sounds and scents are strong triggers for memories. Let's say that in your session you played a certain CD, placed an eye pillow on your client's eyes, infused your massage lubricant with an essential oil, or used a special foot balm while massaging the client's feet. Those are all items clients can purchase for home use; every time they feel, smell, or hear those items, they most likely are transported back to the last time they experienced them—which was a state of relaxation on your table.

Although it isn't the same as receiving a treatment from you, it certainly helps extend the benefits of your work in-between sessions. Depending on the type of work that you do and your clients' goals, some of the products for home use can also be for a direct therapeutic result, such as keeping muscles loose, addressing trigger points, increasing flexibility, or reducing pain.

Regardless of the reasons clients work with you, it's nice when they leave with that "AAAAHHH" feeling. You can extend that feeling of bliss by sending your clients home with products. Spas understand this; they garner a large percentage of income from product sales. Because you are educating clients on self-care rather than doing hard sales, you can sell retail products as part of your practice just like spas in your area do.

As a bonus, retailing can actually increase the frequency of clients booking sessions. When clients use a product at home, it reminds them of the treatment they received, and that often inspires them to book another session. Plus, if they share those products with friends, those friends are more likely to become clients.

The Four Requirements to Effectively Extend Session Benefits:
1. Properly assess clients' needs.
2. Take the time to match potential products with those needs.
3. Educate clients on the proper use of those products.
4. Inspire clients to use the products at home. Make suggestions as to how and when they should do so.

# The Importance of Retailing

Traditionally, the three major ways to increase revenue in your practice are: increase the number of clients you see by working more (or hiring other practitioners to work for you); raise your prices; increase the amount you sell (in services and products) to the same number of clients.

Increasing the amount you sell can easily be done with add-on services, gift certificates, and product sales. One of my favorite sayings is "Do the Math!" Let's say that you have a client base of 100 people. If you sell $50 in products to each client per year, that would increase your income by $5,000. After you factor in the cost of the goods, shipping, promotion, and time, you should still see a net profit of at least $2,000. That's pretty good for just stocking a few items that your clients like and would probably buy something similar from another company anyway. Now imagine bringing in a few higher-end items or increasing the average amount that you sell each year.

## Spas Do it – So Should You

Many spas require their practitioners to sell products. They know that retailing is a critical element in client satisfaction and rely on the income generated by product sales. They know that the sales volume increases when the practitioners have input on the products carried and the products are within the practitioner's scope of practice. Spa retail sales account for about twenty percent of a spa's total revenue, although that percentage greatly increases if the spa carries cosmetology products.[ii] The profit margin on products is typically higher than services. Thus, even a small increase in the revenue from retail sales can make a tremendous difference in the spa's bottom line.

The common expectation is that practitioners generate between 10 to 20 percent of their total sales in home-care products or supplies. Most estheticians, however, are required to generate upwards of 50 percent for their shop. Salaries, bonuses, and seniority are often based on the amount of products sold.

As a side note: Before taking a job at one of these establishments, clarify their product sales requirements, and make sure that you feel comfortable and confident with their product lines. If you currently work in such a setting and don't like the products, then talk with management. Offer input on the product lines so that the company can carry items you feel comfortable selling. This makes it a win/win/win situation for you, the clients, and the company. Perhaps you can help develop a different system so that you don't feel like you are hawking products or rushed for time.

## Sales Reluctance

Some practitioners are reluctant to sell products. One concern relates to "pushing" products, a hard sell. If you view products as an extension of the treatment and a value-added service, sales become a natural part of the client/practitioner relationship (without pressure), particularly when you use the product within the session.

The lack of product knowledge is another aspect that contributes to sales reluctance. Alleviate this reluctance by knowing the major details of the product and its application. Take advantage of training if it's available; if not, read the materials that accompany the products and research the items online.

Retailing does have its challenges, particularly determining what products to sell, how much inventory to carry, the potential to get stuck with stuff that nobody wants, product aging/loss of potency, and schlepping products if you have a mobile practice.

Retailing takes a time investment on your part to thoroughly learn the products, deal with increased paperwork, collect and remit sales tax, create attractive displays, and market the products.

Another common concern is not having enough time between sessions to sell products. Whenever possible, schedule at least 15 minutes between sessions. This allows you time to discuss questions with clients, review their treatment plans, sell appropriate products, and book the next session. When you consider the revenue those 15 minutes generates, how can you afford not to allot that extra time?

**Retailing is a key way to work smarter—not harder!**

## Advantages and Disadvantages of Retailing

**Disadvantages**:
- Doing extra paperwork
- Collecting and remitting sales tax
- Handling inventory management
- Investing time and energy

**Advantages**:
- Adding value to your sessions
- Extending the benefits at home
- Providing convenience to your clients
- Increasing your bottom line

# 2
# Ethical Concerns

Some practitioners fear they will be seen as unprofessional or unethical if they sell products; they want to be respectful and not cross boundaries. The reality is, appropriate product sales actually boosts professionalism. Ethical product sales is not about hype or "hard-sell" tactics. The income you receive from the items your clients purchase is not going to make you rich; on the other hand it can be a decent source of supplemental (passive) income. The point is to provide your clients with easy access to high-quality products that enrich their wellbeing.

Unethical practices, such as aggressive sales techniques or misinformation, have perennially characterized product sales. Fortunately, in the massage and bodywork profession, this is the exception rather than the rule. Nevertheless, you need to be cautious when selling products.

If product sales are not handled well, they can negatively impact your practice. The major issue here is: are you influenced more by the money that product sales generate, or are you selling products to clients because they need or want them? Exercise caution and check your motives to make certain that you are not "pushing" a little harder because your income is down or because you are required to meet a targeted sales volume.

A conflict doesn't need to exist as long as a few guidelines are followed. If you currently run a professional, ethical practice, then retailing can naturally follow suit. If you keep good boundaries, treat people with respect and fairness, and remain client-centered, you will manage product sales in the same manner as the rest of your practice.

# The Power Differential

The power differential is the key factor in ethical product sales. As a wellness practitioner, a power differential exists between you and your clients. You are the authority figure whose actions, by virtue of your role, directly affects your clients' well-being. In massage, the power differential is amplified by the physical aspects of practice. Clients take a position—usually lying or sitting—in which they allow you access to their body. You position yourself within the client's physical space, often leaning over the client. Furthermore, in massage, the client is partially or fully unclothed. Although draping is used for privacy, the psychological effect of the unclothed client and the clothed practitioner increases the imbalance of power. Finally, as your hands make physical contact with the client's body, their physical safety is literally in your hands.

Clients may feel uncomfortable about raising concerns or making requests. They may find it difficult to say "no" or refrain from communicating anything that could possibly be construed as negative for fear of reprisal or loss. Clients may feel influenced to purchase products out of a need to please you or because they think you know best. Even if you take great care not to exploit this power differential, it still exists.

Don't manipulate or coerce your clients. It's one thing to display a product, mention it in your marketing materials, or use that product in the session. It's crucial that you invite clients to see if they are interested in learning more about a product. Don't assume that they are interested.

Reduce the possible abuse of the power differential by restricting your conversation about products to before or after sessions. It's fine to mention the product during a session, such as, "Now I am going to use XYZ product on you. If you are interested in learning more information about it, we can discuss it after the session."

The post-session interview is a good time to reference products. It is natural to recommend products that are appropriate to the client's goals when you are reviewing the treatment plan and any "homework" you might have for a client. It is also the time to ask for feedback on any of the products you used during the session.

Actually, when your selection of sell-thru products closely relates to your session, product recommendation becomes easier. Give your clients the power to learn more about maintaining their health and making better decisions. Remember that you are simply providing a solution for your clients.

Researchers at Columbia University found that states of relaxation increase customers' sense of what a product is worth, often by as much as 10 percent.[iii] According to one of the researchers Michael Tuan Pham,

> The study reveals a psychological reaction to the biology of being relaxed: Your system thinks there is no threat in the environment. As a result, you tend to perceive various things as more desirable. Shoppers should be aware of how this impacts their decision-making.

According to the report, relaxed consumers think products are worth more than less-relaxed consumers because relaxed individuals tend to think about the value of products at a more abstract level. For example, when assessing the monetary value of a digital camera, compared to less-relaxed consumers, more-relaxed consumers would tend to focus more on what the camera will enable them to do (e.g., collect memories) and how desirable and advantageous it is to own it, as opposed to the concrete features of the camera itself (e.g., the number of megapixels, the lens zoom range), its potential disadvantages, and the practicality of its purchase. The phenomenon appears to reflect an inflation of value by relaxed individuals rather than a deflation of value by less-relaxed individuals.

# Product Knowledge

Ethical sales are based upon educating your clients on the benefits of certain products and allowing them the opportunity to purchase them from you. Only sell products that you know are reliable, suitable for use by your clients, within your scope of practice, a natural extension of your business, and congruent with your image. Choose items that are professional grade and reliable. Remember, you have access to products that most consumers can't easily find! Note that sometimes companies offer products to the general consumer market that are not the same formulation as professional grade. If some of the products you sell fall into this category, you need to describe the differences to your clients.

Clients depend on you to provide them with accurate information and guidance. You must know every one of your products well. Take the time to do research so you can properly educate clients. For instance, if your client really enjoyed the cervical hot pack you used during the session and wants to purchase one, educate the client on how to use the pack and under what circumstances not to use it.

Your clients will lose faith in you (and then no longer be your clients, not to mention the loss of goodwill) if you fail to adequately inform them about the appropriate use, benefits, limitations, and possible side effects or contraindications of the products you sell. As a side note, don't make product claims that the manufacturer doesn't make or would not support (aka: "snake oil" claims).

# Nutritional Supplements

In your quest to diversify your practice, you might consider selling nutritional supplements. The major concern is that you may be beyond your scope of practice, unless you are a nutritionist or herbalist (or extremely well versed in this subject).

We have been in some wellness practitioners' offices where the waiting room looks like a small health food store. It is highly unlikely that those practitioners know much about all the various products they carry. You might be thinking that store clerks don't know that information either, so what's the problem? Essentially, the problem is that you have a client/practitioner relationship, which differs from a consumer/retailer relationship.

But what if a product has changed your life, or someone you know has experienced profound change using that product? How can you *not* sell it? After all, your role is to support your clients in their overall wellness. If there's a product that you really trust and want to offer to your clients, educate yourself on the product: the contents, its suggested applications, possible adverse reactions, and contraindications. Keep in mind that just because a product works for you doesn't mean it is beneficial to the next person.

Beware: "Works for me" is a tricky phrase. Be very wary of anecdotal evidence. Results aren't always proven or reliable. The possibility exists that the product could even be harmful to someone else. When discussing nutritional supplements with clients, you need to discuss the potential side effects in addition to explaining the benefits.

The more informed you are about the products you carry, the less risk there is for you and your clients. If you are interested in herbs and vitamins, consider taking courses on the subject—or even pursue a degree in nutrition or herbology. Another option to help ensure that you are providing your clients with information and products that are in their best interest is to team up with a nutritionist or herbalist.

The U.S. market is flooded with nutritional supplements; it is a market that is largely unregulated. The general public is looking for direction. As wellness providers, your clients naturally rely upon you to provide them with information, products and services to enhance their well-being.

Proceed cautiously when it comes to selling nutritional supplements and always work within your scope of practice and knowledge.

## Ethical Do's and Don'ts

### Ethical Product Sales: Do's

- Make sure the products you carry are appropriate and wanted.
- Find products that meet clients'goals and needs.
- Know the products well.
- Educate your clients on the proper use, benefits, and possible side-effects.
- Restrict discussion of products to before or after the session.
- Ask for client feedback.
- Clearly label the cost of products.

### Ethical Product Sales: Don'ts

- Don't overuse products.
- Don't make product claims that the manufacturer doesn't make.
- Don't manipulate or coerce your clients.

# 3
# Choose Appropriate Products

There are so many products that you can sell. You just need to make sure there aren't any local statutes or specific industry guidelines forbidding the sale of certain items. In addition to healthcare products designed to assist in the relief of pain and promote well-being, it's fine to sell ancillary items that are fun or make for unique gifts. Selling products that help clients feel pampered (and who doesn't need that from time to time?) is also appropriate. Just imagine how lovely it would be for your clients to create a mini-oasis of tranquility in their homes.

We've interviewed many people on the types of products they sell and what seems to work best. The most successful items are those that help clients with their pain issues, home self-care products, and gift items.

The tricky part is balance. Your retail offerings should be modest unless you have a bustling office with numerous practitioners, a large waiting area where you can display a lot of products, and a front desk person to process orders.

According to a survey of massage therapists commissioned by MASSAGE Magazine, and conducted by Lewis & Clark survey company in 2013, more than one-quarter of respondents currently make retail sales of products to their massage therapy clients and more than one third are interested in learning how to do so. Among those respondents who currently make retail sales, the most frequently sold products are analgesics and topicals, essential oils, and aromatherapy products.

# Types of Products Sold to Massage Therapy Clients:[iv]

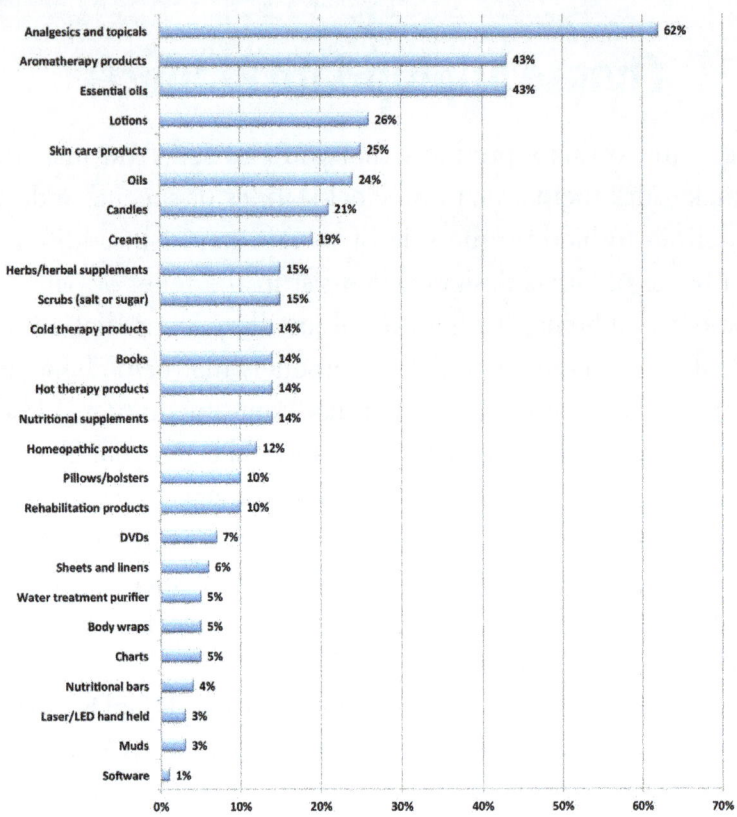

| Product | Percentage |
|---|---|
| Analgesics and topicals | 62% |
| Aromatherapy products | 43% |
| Essential oils | 43% |
| Lotions | 26% |
| Skin care products | 25% |
| Oils | 24% |
| Candles | 21% |
| Creams | 19% |
| Herbs/herbal supplements | 15% |
| Scrubs (salt or sugar) | 15% |
| Cold therapy products | 14% |
| Books | 14% |
| Hot therapy products | 14% |
| Nutritional supplements | 14% |
| Homeopathic products | 12% |
| Pillows/bolsters | 10% |
| Rehabilitation products | 10% |
| DVDs | 7% |
| Sheets and linens | 6% |
| Water treatment purifier | 5% |
| Body wraps | 5% |
| Charts | 5% |
| Nutritional bars | 4% |
| Laser/LED hand held | 3% |
| Muds | 3% |
| Software | 1% |

## Product Ideas:

- Air purifiers
- Air purifying sprays
- Bath salts
- Body butters
- Books
- Candles
- CDs
- DVDs
- Dry Brushes
- Ergonomic devices
- Essential oils
- Eye pillows
- Facial lotions
- Foot balms
- Gifts items
- Greeting cards
- Hot and cold packs
- Jewelry
- Kinesiology tape
- Lip balms

- Locally made tinctures
- Oils/lotions/creams/ gels
- Pain erasure balls
- Relaxation tools
- Scrubs
- Self-care items
- Self-massage tools
- Slippers
- Stretching bands
- Sunscreen
- Support pillows
- Tape
- Topical analgesics
- Yoga gear

Carefully consider the products you sell. Select products with a healthy profit margin, are beneficial, you believe in, and your clients need or want (the BUS). When choosing the right product, ideally choose one that is NOT commonly sold, is unique, and if possible, is an extension of your work. Occasionally you might carry an item that is easy to find, but you make it available for convenience—so that you client doesn't need to make a stop on the way home. A prime example of this is Epsom salts. Many practitioners recommend clients go home and take an Epsom Salt bath after the session—particularly after a vigorous session or if the client had a lot of holding patterns or trigger points.

## Product Research

Research is the first step in determining which products to carry. Start with identifying the retail products that correspond to the specific services you provide. Next get feedback from clients. Become familiar with the details of the potential products. Ask other practitioners for their input. The final step is to purchase products and test them yourself.

Look for quality items. Just because something costs less doesn't make it a better value. When comparing similar products, the more expensive item might be made from higher quality ingredients, last longer, or need less to be just as effective.

### Match Your Services with Products

Create a 3-column document. Label the columns "Services," "Service Products," and "Client Products." List the services you offer in the first column. Put any corresponding products you actually use with each specific service in the second column. In the third column, identify the types of retail products that could complement each service. When you do this, you might find that some of the items in columns 2 and 3 are the same for multiple services. This is a good thing, as it increases the chances of clients buying those products.

After you do this initial stage of research, create a 2-column document. Label the columns "Client Goals/Issues" and "Matching Products." Review your clients' files and list their goals and issues; place them in the first column. Match those up with possible items to sell in the second column.

Now, combine both lists. This activity helps you to determine what products to suggest to your clients as well as what additional products you might want to carry.

## Get Client Feedback

Survey your clients as to what they would like you to carry. You might be pleasantly surprised to find out what they are willing to buy from you. Many clients would rather the money they spend on retail items supports their wellness providers than to buy a similar product from a less personal retail establishment.

Here are some options: verbally request feedback during the client's post-session review; give them a survey card that they fill out before they leave (and perhaps give them a 10% discount on any products purchased that day); and send an email survey as a separate mailing or part of your newsletter.

## Attend Expos

Conferences and expos are a great place to see a variety of items that you could sell in your practice. You get to see them, touch them, smell them, and actually use the item or apply the product. Many vendors do demonstrations and even hold mini-training sessions on how to use and sell their products. You can usually get free samples of products and deep discounts when you purchase items at these events.

### Read Labels Carefully

Product labels can be misleading. For instance, "Natural" (and especially "All Natural") doesn't really mean anything; "organic" products might contain chemicals; "hypoallergenic" products still might irritate someone's skin; and "fragrance-free" products might emanate scents (even though no additional scents were added).

### Review Product Information Sheets

Manufacturers usually supply detailed product information sheets. You can get them sent to you directly, or in many cases you can download them from the company's website. Sometimes you can find videos on how to use the product. Look for their warranty information.

### Talk to Colleagues

Ask your fellow practitioners about their experiences with certain products. Get feedback on how their clients liked (or disliked) certain items, which items sell best, how they market their retailing, and where they buy their products. Keep in mind that everyone has their own preferences and biases; talking with other practitioners can provide you with great insights.

### Buy in Small Quantities at First

Buying in small quantities is a safer way to experiment with retailing. The disadvantage is that your profit margin won't be very large. Still, it's better than having products that just sit on the shelf. Keep track of what items sell quickly and then you can increase your purchases of those products.

## Offer Samples

Many companies provide free or low-cost trial packets/sachets and small-sized samplers. Samples are a great way to introduce clients to the products you use in treatments as well as items for home-care. And clients love to get free product samples. Look for companies that offer pre-packed samples for you and always give samples with something containing your business name and phone number to remind clients where they received the sample.

Consider putting a sticker with a nominal price on those samples (such as 75 cents or a dollar). This makes clients feel special when you actually give the client a sample at no charge (you never actually charge anyone for the samples). Clients appreciate the gesture and as a bonus it discourages clients from grabbing handfuls of free samples. The great thing about sampling is that if a client tries and likes a product, it sells itself!

## Test the Product

Know how to use any product you sell. Something might sound good on paper, but could be cumbersome to use, smells weird, has unfortunate side-effects, or isn't very effective.

First, test the product on yourself. Next, ask a few key clients to test the product. Give the testers a form to fill out that asks questions about their experience with the product. In addition to helping you ascertain if you should carry a specific product, their feedback can help you determine how to market it and the depth of client education needed. Anita Shannon of ACE Massage Cupping states,

> This is also a wonderful way to collect testimonials and before-and-after photos in advance and include them in your presentation materials. In client retention, a photo really is worth a thousand words. [v]

# Distributors

Financial success in retailing requires that you purchase products at wholesale prices and mark up those prices appropriately. Many practitioners purchase items from a distributor that carries a wide selection from a variety of manufacturers. Sometimes practitioners buy bulk products directly from a manufacturer or publisher. You might get a better price if you go directly to the manufacturer, although it's rare, and the minimum purchase quantity may be prohibitive. Most manufacturers only sell through distributors as they prefer to work with companies that buy hundreds or thousands of units of their product at a time. Some manufacturers might offer you free items and sales support materials. You can usually receive those items even if you don't directly purchase products from them.

The main benefits of buying from a distributor are that you only have to place one order for multiple product lines, and the minimum quantity orders might be more flexible than the manufacturer's requirements. If you are just starting out and can't afford the minimum, consider joining forces with other practitioners and make cooperative purchases.

Whenever possible, work with companies that provide marketing materials (e.g., brochures, eye-attracting posters, point-of-sale displays) and samples for a nominal cost, or better yet, for free! Some companies provide these types of items for free while others charge a fee or provide them for free with a minimum order.

For instance, Performance Health is an excellent example of a manufacturer that supports practitioners who sell their products—even though the practitioners actually purchase the products through one of their distributors. They provide a full suite of free marketing assistance for their line of Biofreeze Pain Reliever products: customized brochures with your name and phone number with one 5-gram trial packets attached; countertop displays; window decals; free samples for volunteer events; a "Find a Professional" function on their website that lists your office's name, address, website, products you sell, and hours of operation.

Choose companies that understand the nuances of the massage and bodywork industry and actively support this industry. Look for companies (and products) that have worked to brand themselves and are consumer driven.

Some of the other considerations to factor in your choice of companies are: their level of customer service; how quickly product is shipped; how shipping charges are assessed; what are their return policies; do they offer the best price; and do they provide price guarantees.

Ideally, work with companies that have a social consciousness; those that are concerned about the quality, sustainability, and the environmental impact of the production of their products. Ask the company representative to explain any of the ingredients or technological issues that you don't fully understand, and ask other pertinent questions like: the common uses of the product, contraindications, complaints, and shelf life.

## How to Set Up An Account

Most distributors offer a bulk discount to any practitioner, which still provides a reasonable profit margin. However, practitioners who sign up for a reseller account usually receive an additional 15-20% discount. The process of setting up an account with a distributor varies by company. The majority require you to fill out an application and supply credit references (although references are usually waived if you are prepaying for the purchases). There is usually a minimum order, either in total cost or quantity. This varies greatly by company. Some also require a minimum annual amount. Note that some distribution companies have their own private labelled products and those discounts are often deeper.

## Links to Distributors:

- Massage Warehouse (http://www.massagewarehouse.com/)
- Universal Companies (http://www.universalcompanies.com/)
- Spa & Bodywork Market (http://www.spabodyworkmarket.com/)
- Orthopedic Physical Therapy Products (http://www.optp.com/)
- Yoga Direct (http://www.yogadirect.com/)
- 360 Fitness Superstore (http://www.360fitnesssuperstore.com/)

Note: Readers of *Retail Mastery* can receive exclusive discounts (https://ya250.infusionsoft.com/app/page/retail-mastery-resources) from some of these distributors.

## A Twist on Traditional Sales

Traditional sales involve a practitioner buying products at wholesale and reselling to clients. This involves an investment of time and money. Here are two creative ways to work with manufacturers or distributors (particularly for high-end items).

Display the item. Clients place orders through the practitioner (and the item is either delivered directly to the client or the practitioner). This involves some time and paperwork, but lessens your financial risk.

Display the item, provide clients with order information, clients order directly from the manufacturer, and the manufacturer sends you a commission check. (This option takes almost no time and incurs no risk.)

# Private Labeling

Do you have an idea for a product that you would like to use in your practice and offer to sell to your clients, but you haven't found exactly what you want? If so, consider creating a private-label product. In addition to controlling what you want in the product, having your own label fosters customer loyalty and  boosts retail sales. Some practitioners private-label small batch items (e.g., soaps, scrubs) for special events. Keep in mind that these type of items generally have a limited shelf life.

Private Labeling is a great marketing tool. If a client has purchased any type of product with your name and contact information on it, this makes it easier for that client to contact you to rebook a session or order more products.

Private-label products can also be a source of referrals. For instance, a client purchases a private-labeled product from you and gives it as a gift. The recipient now has your contact information on an item that came from a trusted source (the friend).

Note: Most practitioners who do private-label products limit it to less than five items. If you want to create a customized product, first research brand names to verify your brand and trademark are unique.

### Links to Bottles and Jars:

- Bottles and More (http://www.bottlesandmore.com/)
- C. L. Smith (http://www.clsmith.com/)
- Wheaton (http://wheaton.com/primary-packaging/glass.html)

- Drug & Cosmetic Packaging (http://www.pumpking.com/)
- Container & Packaging Supply
  (https://www.containerandpackaging.com/)
- McKernan Packaging Clearing House (https://mckernan.com/)
- Specialty Bottle (https://www.specialtybottle.com/)
- SKS Bottle & Packaging (https://www.sks-bottle.com/)
- Berlin Packaging (https://www.berlinpackaging.com/)

## Private Label Companies

Private labeling isn't limited to creating new products. Some companies will put your labels on their products. Contact the manufacturers of your favorite products to see if they offer private labeling. Do a web search for those companies. Here is a list of some that we found:

### Links to Private Label Companies:

- Prima Fleur (http://www.primafleur.com/private_label.php)
- Innovative Body Science (http://www.innovativebodyscience.com/)
- Private Label Products (http://www.privatelabelproducts.us/)
- Pravada (https://pravadaprivatelabel.com/)
- Bulk Apothecary
  (http://www.bulkapothecary.com/private-label-massage-lotion/)
- Aroma Terra (http://www.aromaterra.com/massage-lotions.html)
- Artisan Aromatics
  (https://artisanessentialoils.com/essential-oil-private-labeling/)
- Nectarine (http://www.storenectarine.com/)

Working with a full-service private-label manufacturer is another option. They review the formula, determine the appropriate containers, and the practitioner works with one of their chemists to finalize the formula. Traditionally the manufacturer makes a small test run. After final approval, the product is ready for production (The whole process may take from several days to several months). Full-service manufacturers often have a wide selection of customizable stock products, and offer packaging suggestions, label options, logo design, photography support, legal assistance (e.g., government labeling requirements) and educational resources.

The cost of creating a custom private-label product depends upon the complexity of the formulation, label and packaging design and production, and minimal inventory. This can range from $200 to thousands of dollars.

For liability concerns you will most likely be covered by the manufacturer's insurance policy as long as the manufacturer's name is somewhere on the label (check with the manufacturer to be sure). If you produce these items in-house, you must make sure that you have the appropriate liability insurance.

## Product Liability

Most manufacturers guarantee their products against harm from proper use. The gray area is when you as a practitioner use a product on a client. Protect yourself by carrying sufficient malpractice and product liability insurance coverage.

For instance, the MASSAGE Magazine Insurance Plus program (MMIP) (https://www.massageliabilityinsurancegroup.com/professional-2/) includes product liability covering claims made against you for damage or injury resulting from a product you use on clients. Their coverage is $2 million per occurrence and $2 million annual aggregate.

Keep in mind that once a client uses a product themselves, your product liability insurance does not cover any claims. Clients would need to make a claim directly against the manufacturer.

# 4
# Financial Management

The financial management of retail sales includes pricing products, controlling inventory, and complying with sales tax requirements. Software programs and online tools can streamline this process and save you a lot of stress.

## Pricing Products

When it comes to pricing, charge a fair but profitable price. Your distributor or the product's manufacturer should guide you with suggestions of the proper selling prices for products. They will usually provide you with the MSRP (Manufacturer's Suggested Retail Price). it is the price the company suggests you charge for its products. In general, you can charge whatever you want, although some companies may not allow you to sell below the MSRP.

Most retail sales use the keystoning method, which means that you mark up merchandise to an amount that is double the wholesale price. Thus, if you buy a product for $5 then you sell it for $10. You will find that some products offer an even better markup than that. In most instances, you also have to pay shipping and that can add up if the item is heavy.

The cost of selling products is not limited to purchase price and shipping. You must consider the time involved in placing orders, displaying products, and marketing. Also factor in the time to manage the paperwork involved in for collecting sales tax and submitting tax reports.

And then what do you do with inventory that doesn't sell, or ages beyond its "best by" date?

## Inventory Control

Practitioners who sell products need to keep track of what has been ordered, how long it takes to receive merchandise, how long it takes to sell merchandise, and what's in stock. You don't want to run out of your best-selling item—particularly if it takes weeks to obtain more. It isn't wise to carry too much stock that has a relatively short shelf life: oils that can go rancid or magazines that are published monthly.

If you carry a limited selection of products, daily inventory can be checked visually and a written tally (often referred to as a physical inventory) taken at least twice per year.

A more formal approach to inventory is recommended if you stock a wide variety of goods. Most accounting software packages include inventory recordkeeping. These programs keep track of inventory on hand and alert you when stock gets low. The programs can output a variety of reports to track sales trends. This assists you in determining what products to sell and how to sell them.

For instance, if you have only sold 1 unit of a certain product in 6 months, perhaps it should be eliminated from your product line. Also, if you have an item with a quickly approaching expiration date, you might consider reducing the price or giving it away as an added-value promotion.

If you want to test the waters and not invest in software right away, we've created a free inventory spreadsheet (https://ya250. infusionsoft.com/app/page/retail-mastery-resources) that you can adapt and use in Google Sheets or Microsoft Excel.

Forgetting to place an order can easily happen when you're busy with all the other aspects of running a practice. Charting inventory activities reduces the chances for errors and provides you with a quick overview.

Note: even if you rely on computerized inventory control, do a physical inventory at least twice each year, as posting errors can occur and adjustments need to be made.

Another option to manage inventory when you're starting out is to limit the products you carry to a few items until you are more comfortable with the process and are more attuned to what your clients want to purchase. Ideally, you would have products on hand, but if you have major concerns about carrying inventory, have a sign-up sheet where clients place orders. Purchase those items when you've reached the minimum amount needed for a wholesale order. Some wholesalers will drop-ship products directly to your clients.

## Sample Inventory Record:

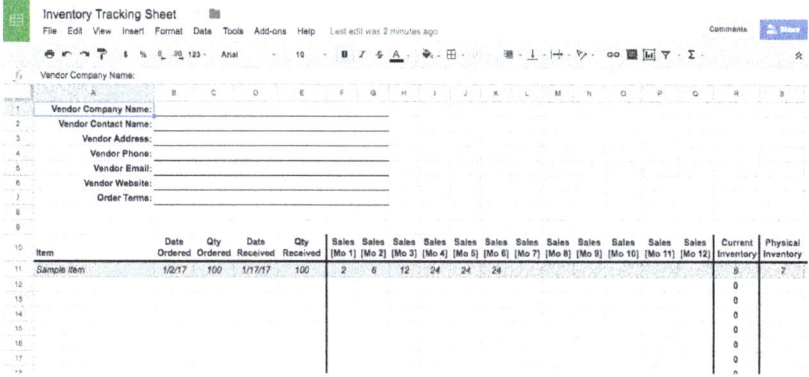

# Sales Tax

Dealing with sales tax is one of the biggest concerns practitioners have about product sales. Visions of stacks of paperwork and endless reels of red tape take over their thoughts. Collecting and remitting sales tax is quite easy to do once you have the proper licenses.

Sales tax is calculated by multiplying the purchase price by the applicable tax rate, and is collected by the seller at the time of sale.

Technically, you don't have to "collect" it: that is the amount you must remit to the government. If you don't charge your clients the sales tax, that money comes out of your pocket.

The U.S. Small Business Administration (SBA) has a great website page for finding licensing requirements. Its Business Licenses and Permits Search Tool allows you to search by location (city, state or zip code), combined with your type of business. Massage is one of the 15 types of business listed! Once you put in the information and select "Search" you get a results page that lists the federal, state and local permits, licenses, and registrations you need to run that business. It also provides links to web pages, contact information, application forms and instructions.

You need a Transaction Privilege Tax License (sometimes called a Resale Permit) if you live in a state that requires you to collect and remit sales tax. Sometimes, a sales tax license is bundled with a Business License. Keep in mind that in most states a Business License is not the same as an Occupational or Professional License. Many states don't even require service businesses to have a Business License; you only need to apply for a Transaction Privilege Tax License.

Contact your State Department of Revenue to apply for a Transaction Privilege Tax License. Some cities and counties require an additional Transaction Privilege Tax License. Discuss tax collection requirements with the state, as well as with the company from which you buy products for resale. If you purchase products to resell, you don't need to pay sales tax to the company that sells you the product. When you order products, the company often asks for your resale number (which is on the Transaction Privilege Tax License).

If you have any difficulty getting the information you need from the above sources, go to your State Department of Revenue (DOR) website. We searched a couple of different states and found that the DOR websites had the most complete, clear information—and included local requirements too.

### Information Needed to Get a Transaction Privilege Tax License:

- Business name
- Business entity (e.g., sole proprietor, LLC, PSC) and date it was established
- Employer ID Number (http://www1.ein-gov.us/) or Social Security Number if you are a sole proprietor with no employees
- The starting date for collecting sales tax in your state
- The type of products or services to be sold
- The amount of sales tax you estimate you will collect
- If you have more than one location, whether you will be filing consolidated returns

## Reports

How often you must submit reports and the collected sales tax can vary. Usually you are required to fill out a form on a monthly basis for the first year. If the volume is low, the state might reduce it to quarterly or even annually. Remember, that while it is called state sales tax, the percentages usually vary by the type of taxable activity and the city.

Now that you know the sales tax rate to charge, you are on your way! If you use an accounting or office-management software program, it should calculate the amount of sales tax to charge for each sale and prepare your sales tax reports.

# 5
# The Art of Selling Products

Selling products is not about hype or "hard-sell" tactics. The income you receive from the items your clients purchase is not going to make you rich, but it can be a decent source of supplemental income.

Just carrying a product doesn't guarantee it will sell. Because people are more inclined to buy something they've experienced, incorporate your products into your practice and take the time to educate your clients. Always keep in mind that the major focus of product sales is providing your clients with easy access to high-quality products that enrich their well-being.

Ultimately, selling products is like "selling" your services—simply share your enthusiasm about them. If you make your products visible, accessible, attractive and affordable, your clients will buy them when it's appropriate.

For those of you who haven't been selling products, we encourage you to give it a try. Start out small and gradually increase the types and quantity of products you carry. For those of you who already are comfortable with product sales, we hope that you revamp what you do, looking for ways to increase those sales and perhaps even work with some higher-ticket items.

Selling products isn't often second nature to practitioners, so setting sales goals can keep you motivated. Ask yourself questions, such as, "How much would I have to do in sales to get [fill in the blank]" This can be done in increments for specific purchases and activities (e.g., buying new equipment, taking a vacation), to long-term commitments, such as hiring an employee or opening a retirement plan. If you have staff, inspire their retail sales efforts by giving some type of reward for meeting their goals (in addition to any commission they would already receive).

There are many ways to incorporate product sales in your practice to support your clients'well-being and the well-being of your bottom line. This section highlights the concepts behind effective retailing, overviews three sales methods, and provides specific suggestions for creative ways to sell products.

# The Four C's of Effective Sales

Building relationships is the foundation of effective sales in massage therapy and bodywork. Consider the Four C's of Communication, Consultation, Convenience, and Compliance in fostering those relationships.

## Communication

Excellent communication skills are the foundation of effective sales. A popular phrase is, "Selling isn't Telling." In fact, selling is first and foremost about listening. Listen to what your clients tell you is important to them; respond in a manner that is educational in nature.

Deftness at artful phrasing and asking clients open-ended questions are skills honed over time. It involves forethought and lots of practice. Open-ended questions facilitate therapeutic communication as they encourage clients to express their thoughts and feelings. Open-ended questions usually begin with how, what, when, why, where, who, which, or could. These types of questions also help the client to feel like an active partner in the treatment process.

In contrast, closed-ended questions are limited in scope, as the answer is usually a simple "yes" or "no." An example of an open-ended questions is, "What products would you like to take home today?" Whereas a close-ended question example is, "Would you like to take home any products today?"

## Consultation

Product recommendation becomes easier when your selection of retail products closely relates to what you do in your sessions. Give your clients the power to learn more about maintaining their health and making better decisions. When you provide the right products to clients, their satisfaction and the value of your advice grows. This is one reason a thorough intake interview and a post-session interview are important.

The intake interview is when you identify clients' concerns and goals. The post-session interview is when you summarize the session, establish the long-term wellness care plan, and recommend any reference materials, relaxation tools, support devices, books, or other items that are appropriate to the client's goals.

Educate your clients about the benefits and features of your products. This can be done with verbal descriptions, demonstrations, signs, literature, brochures, articles, DVDs, and product testers. Most people prefer to smell and feel products before purchasing them.

## Convenience

Clients have the immediate satisfaction of knowing they can obtain and use products recommended by a wellness practitioner. They would rather not have to decide between multiple, unknown products on a retail shelf.

By sending clients home with samples they are more likely to make future purchases when they return for treatment. Keeping your business at the top of clients'minds creates passive revenue that builds your practice.

This is all about time management. Most people are extremely busy. This is where even selling an item that they could easily buy elsewhere is helpful.

## Compliance

You know what treatments work for clients and what they can do to maintain better health. Many of the services you offer aren't completely effective unless you can extend and enhance the benefits you offer in treatment. Self-care is most successful when clients do what a practitioner instructs. When you recommend a product for home use and explain how to apply it (and demonstrate what to do), chances are greater the product will be used properly. Ideally, have clients participate in your demonstration.

The trend is that people are taking a more proactive role in their wellness. When clients purchase products they are actively taking responsibility for some of their own self-care. You might find that clients who purchase products from you are also more likely follow your other recommendations, such as stretching. Remember that you are the expert! By selling clients the right products, they can increase their wellness goals.

# Sales Methods

Let's explore three methods of selling products: recommendations, signature treatments, and direct sales. Most practitioners incorporate a mixture of these methods in their retailing ventures.

## Recommending

Recommending is the most common form of communicating about product sales. It's easy and natural if you've properly assessed your client's needs, and have the appropriate products on hand. And, you avoid suggesting unwanted or unavailable items.

Utilize the products you sell in your sessions: play a CD; apply a hot or cold pack; use specialized gels, creams or liniments; incorporate strength and agility items; or include aromatherapy applications. Later you can easily sell those items to your clients because they have already enjoyed them.

If a client mentions liking anything in your session (e.g., the music you played, the hot pack you put on to the client's back, the topical analgesic you applied to a painful area, the special foot balm you applied, the warmed booties you put on the client's feet), assemble those items on a tray. When the client is checking out, display the tray and say something like, "These are the items that were used in your session and are available if you would like to purchase for use at home." You can also remind the client that she mentioned she liked certain items, state where you used the items, and give a bit more information about some of the products.

Another option is to provide clients with product suggestion sheets. These are handy, particularly if you don't have a lot of time between clients, and are often experienced as less invasive than if you talked directly with the client about the products. Please refer to the sample sheet (see below). You can leave the Product and Activity lines blank, or you could have a master sheet with the most common items already printed and a few blank lines to customize. Either write down the recommended products and instructions or check off key products.

## WELLNESS ASSOCIATES
123 BREEZE • ANYWHERE • 555-5555 WWW.WELLNESSASSOCIATES.COM

| Jane Doe | 3/7 |
|---|---|
| CLIENT NAME | DATE |

### HOME CARE SUGGESTIONS*

| | DAILY AM | DAILY PM | WEEKLY TIMES/WEEK |
|---|---|---|---|
| Product 1  Topical | √ | √ | daily |
| Product 2  Self-Massage Tool | as needed | | |
| Product 3 | | | |
| Product 4 | | | |
| | | | |
| Activity 1  Shoulder Stretches | | √ | daily |
| Activity 2  Relaxation Exercises | | | 3x/week |
| Activity 3 | | | |
| Activity 4 | | | |

*Only add products and activities when appropriate and within your scope of practice.

### FOLLOW-UP CARE / WHEN

| | |
|---|---|
| Next Session | Tues 3/14 |
| Talk to PCP regarding skin condition | ASAP |

Mary Massage, LMT
PRACTITIONER

*Sample Product Recommendation borrowed with permission from Business Mastery, 5th edition* (http://businessmastery.us/). *Readers of Retail Mastery can download a free Product Recommendation Sheet* (https://ya250.infusionsoft.com/app/page/retail-mastery-resources).

## Signature Treatments

A Signature Treatment consists of bundling a combination of services and products. Offering signature treatments is one of the easiest ways to indirectly increase your product sales as well as encourage bookings as they generate client excitement and anticipation for the next special. Give them fun titles that spark your clients' curiosity. Create elaborate packages that include a special routine and even some customized scrubs or aromatherapy blends. Consider having a at least one ongoing signature treatment and then offering rotating, limited-time treatments on a monthly or quarterly basis.

Publicize these treatments with posters in your office; include announcements in your newsletters and email blasts. Ideally, include photos of the products you are including in the treatment.

When the session is over, show the clients the products you used and ask if they would like to purchase any to take home.

An option for Signature Treatments is to "Bake" in products. Baking is done by creating a Signature Treatment that includes using a product(s) in the session and the client takes the remainder of the product(s) home. This approach takes the stress out of selling. It is also an excellent strategy if you employ therapists, as the therapists can focus on the treatment and don't have to be concerned about selling.

A simple example of a signature treatment with baked in products is the "Weekend Warrior Pain Relief Treatment" that includes an 90-minute massage with the use of a topical analgesic and a hot pack. After the treatment, the client goes home with the remainder of the topical analgesic and the hot pack.

Let's say that your normal 90-minute session rate is $100. The retail price of the topical is $15 and the retail price of the heat pack is $20, for a total of $35; your cost for the products is $17.50. You set the price for this special treatment at $125. The client saves $10 and you earn enough to make a profit. It's a Win/Win experience for everyone. Plus, by including a product that needs replenishing, and the client really likes it, you have set it up for ongoing sales.

Bon Vital' (http://www.bonvital.com/) has many detailed examples of Signature Treatments and monthly special treatments that include: a listing of the products needed, a step-by-step description of the routine, a breakdown of the cost, and a suggested retail price. Some of those examples also include a list of the items to be "baked." Please note that many of the examples include other items that you could have the client take home, such as an eye mask. Plus you can adapt these treatments to add other products.

Here's a signature treatment from Bon Vital' created by Katie Haley, LMT, Debbie Kirsch, LMT, and Lynda Solien-Wolfe, LMT, called the Massagearita Signature Treatment (http://www.bonvital. com/media/wysiwyg/bonVital/treatmentGuides/massagearita.pdf):

**Description:** This is a tropical, refreshing, and stimulating aromatherapy massage for the mind and body! Sure to take you to St. Somewhere!

**Time:** 60 minutes

**Cost per Treatment:** $18.60 (Treatment $3.60 + Take Home Products $15.00)

**Suggested Charge per Treatment:** $85-$125

**Products Needed:**
- Bon Vital' Coconut Oil
- Bon Vital' Lime Essential Oil
- Bon Vital' Sweet Orange Essential Oil
- Bon Vital' Lime Roll-on Essential Oil
- TheraPearl "Eye-ssential" Mask (chilled)
- 2 oz. plastic or glass bottle
- Several warm, moist towels

## Aromatherapy Recipe

To prepare the signature Massagearita Oil, add 10 drops of Lime Essential Oil and 2 drops of Orange Essential Oil to 2 oz of Coconut Oil. Gently shake to combine the oils.

# KEY INGREDIENTS

Coconut Oil

Lime

Sweet Orange

## Treatment Instructions

Begin with your client in supine position:

1. **The Face & Scalp**. Add a few drops of Massagearita oil in your hand, rub together and hold above your client's face for them to inhale, taking 3 long deep breaths. Begin Swedish Massage treatment with gentle effleurage strokes to the face, moving in an upward direction, firm circular motions to temples and scalp. Place the chilled eye mask on your client.

2. **The Upper Extremities**. Move on to the neck and trapezius. Be sure to include some gentle stretches for the neck. Massage each arm.

3. **The Lower Extremities**. Massage each leg beginning with the feet. Apply Lime roll-on essential oil to the bottom of each foot.

4. Turn client to prone position:

5. **The Back**. Turn down sheet to client's hip and place a warm towel infused with Lime essential oil on client's back. Use compression strokes over warm towel beginning at the trapezius and work down the back. Remove the towel while still warm. Apply Massagearita oil with effleurage stroke and complete a Swedish massage—back, arms, then legs. As you finish each leg, end with a long gliding stroke from the ankle, up the leg, over the glutes and back, rounding off at the shoulder and coming back down the arm and hands to the leg. Complete the stroke by lifting off at the ankle. Then adjust top sheet over the client.

6. **The Finish**. End the massage with gentle rocking strokes along each side of the body.

7. **Take Home**. The cost of the eye mask and the Lime roll-on essential oil is baked into the treatment cost. Send home

with your client to encourage them to continue their spa experience.

By the way, they also have variations of this treatment: Massagearita Frozen, Massagearita on the Rocks, and Massagearita with Salt. For more ideas, visit these Bon Vital' pages:

- Bon Vital' Signature Treatments
  (http://www.bonvital.com/education/signature-treatments)
- Bon Vital' Treatment of the Month
  (http://www.bonvital.com/education/treatment-of-the-month)

## Direct Selling

Direct selling requires taking a proactive role in marketing your products. Directly inform your clients about your products. Post signs in your office. I've even seen practitioners post product-specific flyers in their restrooms. Print flyers that describe all the products you carry; give these to your clients; mail them (or email digital versions) for special promotions. Mention product sales in your newsletter. Send email blasts about any new product you carry or if you are running a special. (You might consider setting up email marketing campaigns with a marketing automation service.) Promote your products on your website and Social Media sites. Create educational videos and post them on YouTube. (While you don't have to take online orders, it's wise to let people know about the items they can purchase from you.) You can also place ads in specialty publications read by your target markets and on specific social media pages.

### Links to Marketing Automation Services:

- MailChimp (https://mailchimp.com/)
- Constant Contact (https://www.constantcontact.com/index.jsp)
- Get Response (https://www.getresponse.com/)
- AWeber (https://www.aweber.com/)

- Campaign Monitor (https://www.campaignmonitor.com/)
- Mailer Lite (https://www.mailerlite.com/)
- Active Campaign (http://www.activecampaign.com/)
- Vertical Response (http://www.verticalresponse.com/)
- Marketing 360 (https://www.marketing360.com/)

# Creative Ideas for Selling Products

Have fun with retailing! As with any type of marketing, the more interesting you make it, the more likely you are to do it, and the more likely it will be effective. Several creative ideas for selling products include: spotlighting products, bundling products, speaking engagements, hosting an event, starting a product review club, and using social media.

## Spotlight Products

Choose a limited number of products to highlight on a monthly basis. Put those items on a focus area in your waiting room or a tray in your office, make a sign about the special product(s), and mention your top products in your promotional materials.

Use products throughout your office building. For example, if you carry a line of soaps or lotions, place them in the bathroom for your clients to use. Always display a retail sized product in your treatment room. While you may have an extra large bottle of lotion that you use in sessions, nicely display the actual size bottle that a client is more likely to purchase.

Other ideas that can inspire a client to purchase that product are: provide a complimentary spritz of aromatherapy (get permission first, as many people are scent-sensitive); or diffuse an essential oil during the treatment.

## Bundle Products

Bundling products together with other products or certificates is an effective sales technique. These bundles can be designed for clients to purchase for themselves or to give as gifts. People are

You can also create seasonal bundles. This could be for holidays, the actual seasons (winter, spring, summer, or fall), or health-related seasons (e.g., flu season). Consider pairing items that you sell in your practice along with other festive items. For instance, in February (Valentine's Day) you could bundle a self-care tool, an essential oil, a mug, and chocolate.

When assembling bundles, offer a variety of packages that range in price, so your clients can feel good about the purchase while staying in their financial comfort zone. Consider putting together a basic kit that costs approximately $25, a pampering kit in the $50 range, and a deluxe kit that costs $100 or more.

If a gift certificate for your services isn't included in the kit, make a sign that encourages people to add a certificate. Your $50 kit could say something like, "$50 for the kit. Add a gift certificate for a 1-hour session for only $50 more!"

Package the products attractively. You can use baskets or pretty bags. Sometimes simply attaching a ribbon makes a purchase seem special.

## Public Speaking

Include products whenever you host open houses, or give public presentations or demonstrations. These can be part of the presentation itself, where you explain how those products align with your work. Educate the audience about the products. Ideally, you would have the participants experience the products. After the presentation, the participants can purchase those items. Even if the products aren't an integral part of your presentation, you could simply have a nice product display for people to look at before and after the presentation (and hopefully purchase).

We offer a number of prsentation kits—*Managing Stress, Chair Massage, Beginner's Massage*—at our website (https://sohnen-moe. com/prodinfo/presentation-kits.php).

## Host a Product Education and Sampling Event

Engage your clients and their friends by hosting a product education and sampling event. This can be to showcase a new product (or product line) or to spotlight products to help with specific conditions. You can even do this as a mini-workshop.

You could have an event that focuses on reducing holiday stress. Provide an educational segment with facts and tips for managing stress, then follow it up with a sampling of specific stress-reducing items you have for sale, as well as some suggestions for gifts.

## Start a Product Review Club

Start a product review club as a follow-up to your Product Education and Sampling Event, or as a completely separate offering. People love sampling products and sharing their input. This group can meet in person or you can create a discussion group on Facebook or LinkedIn. This is an effective way to get people interested in what you carry and might even introduce you to other products to add to your retail offerings.

## Social Media Marketing

Promote products via social networking (e.g., Facebook Business Page, Twitter, Pinterest, LinkedIn), your website, affiliate sites, and email blasts (e.g., online client newsletters, announcements). This affords you the opportunity to go into depth about a product, include a full-color photo of the items, and even engage in conversation about the items. A great way to boost your placement is to create short YouTube videos that you post on your social media sites.

The key to successful social networking is to build relationships. When posting about products in social networking sites, talk about why you use the product, list the benefits, and include testimonials from clients. Engage your readers. Do surveys, pose questions, and ask for feedback and ideas. Ask your fans and followers to like your page and share the post.

Post on your social media sites whenever you add a new product to your retail line or offer a discount. Be sure to include an ending date to encourage people to take action quickly. If you have an online store on your website, provide discount codes to your social networking groups.

## Holiday Marketing

Many commercial merchandisers start their holiday buying marketing campaigns in September. Then there's the major push with Black Friday (the day after Thanksgiving), Small Business Saturday (the Saturday after Thanksgiving), and Cyber Monday (the Monday after Thanksgiving). Consumers are barraged by the marketing campaigns, decorations, and festivities. As a small business owner, you can ride the coattails of these promotions to generate additional sales for your practice, or to expand your product lines.

Using the National Retail Federation survey data for 2015, FindTheData compiled fascinating facts about the holiday season and included them in the online article, "From Spending to Celebrating: The 2015 Holiday Season in 25 Stats." Here are a few that can help you plan your holiday retail campaign.

- The average person spent approximately $800 during the holidays ($600 on gifts for others, $200 on decorations and food).
- 77% of people took advantage of deals for themselves.
- 46% of holiday shopping happened online with 21% of shoppers using mobile devices.
- More than 50% of people actually want gift cards.

While some people are savvy shoppers and purchase gifts throughout the year, the majority wait to buy their gifts until the holiday season is in full swing. The following chart illustrates when consumers start their holiday shopping.

|  | WOMEN | MEN |
|---|---|---|
| before September | 15.8% | 9.3% |
| September | 8.2% | 5.3% |
| October | 21% | 19.5% |
| November | 39.9% | 43.3% |
| first 2 weeks December | 12.7% | 18.4% |
| last 2 weeks December | 2.4% | 4.2% |

Taken from National Retail Federation survey data for 2015.

The holiday season can be stressful and choosing holiday gifts can be mind boggling. Provide retail options for your clients that make it easy for them to give to friends and family. Offer gift options in several price ranges: $10-$20; $25-$50; $55-$100; $100+. Your retail display should offer ready-to-give products that are visually appealing (see the Holiday Merchandising section in the next chapter). You can bundle packages with items that you might not normally sell during the rest of the year, such as small boxes of local organic chocolates, CDs with instrumental holiday music, mugs, holiday spice blend teas, and hot cocoa mix. You could even sell products that evoke the smell of the holidays, such as pumpkin pie or cinnamon.

You can effectively generate new clients with these retail packages by including a business card and an invitation for an open house or a complimentary mini-massage to generate interest.

Whenever you sell retail gift packages, include an option to add a gift certificate for a massage or another service you offer at your office. On the flip side, whenever you sell gift certificates, include a product, such as: a product sample (e.g., a topical analgesic sachet); a small bottle of items you typically sell in larger containers (e.g., essential oil, custom blended scented oil/lotion, or sports cream); a holiday item such as a plant or a candle; or a health-related item such as a stress ball, a self-massage tool, a book, a pocket chart that shows reflexology points, or an eye pillow. By doing this, you provide a means of instant gratification (the recipient can use the product immediately), plus you plant the seed that people can buy wellness products from you.

For Gift Certificate Templates, visit the Sohnen-Moe.com product catalog. (https://sohnen-moe.com/catalog/)

## Holiday Treatments

Holiday retailing need not be limited to gift items clients buy. Keep your practice at the top of your clients' holiday self-care routine by offering unique services and product combinations that meet their holiday needs. Create Holiday Signature Treatments and give them fun titles, such as The Pumpkin Pie Experience, The Ginger Snap, The Candy Cane Treatment, The Hot Chocolate Wrap, Peppermint Flurry, or Winter Wonderland.

Are they crunched for time? If so, offer an express service that helps them unwind quickly and get back to their busy schedule; include a product that they can take with them, like a relaxing essential oil or a soothing CD.

Do they need an escape? Put together a "getaway" package that incorporates several services (e.g., stone massage, reflexology, scalp massage) and spa products they can use at home.

Or keep it simple by offering holiday themed treatments with the scents of the season like cinnamon or cranberry—and sell items with those fragrances.

## Creative Marketing Approach

Announce your holiday specials early and often: promote products via social networking; give talks and mention your specials; take out ads in local publications; place posters in book stores, health food stores, gyms, sports centers, and any place where you can find your target markets; create a holiday gift packages flyer that you give to current and prospective clients (e.g., use photos of your holiday packages and on the back print the benefits, prices, and contact information); post signs in your office (waiting room, dressing area, and restroom); place online and print ads; and send regular or oversized postcards announcing your holiday product and/or service bundles (direct mail is still a very effective tool).

For Postcard Artwork, visit the Sohnen-Moe.com product catalog. (https://sohnen-moe.com/catalog/)

Ideally, start planting seeds of the gift-giving season in September. Keep it simple with a statement in your promotional materials such as, "Avoid the holiday crunch by giving the gift of health. We offer a selection of wellness products and services." As the holiday seasons approach increase your promotional campaigns to full force by the beginning of November.

You can remind people that this is the perfect time to express their gratitude and give thanks with gifts of health. Host your own event on Black Friday. You can even put a fun spin on it by offering mini-sessions (chair massage would be ideal) with a minimum product or gift certificate purchase.

Plan a special promotion for Small Business Saturday. Take advantage of all the general publicity that gets generated for this national event! If you sell products or gift certificates online, you can also design a Cyber Monday campaign.

As the December holidays near, ramp up your campaigns with friendly reminders of how easy it is to get their shopping done at your establishment.

See the next chapter on merchandising for specific holiday display suggestions.

### Links to Small Business Saturday Information:

- Small Business Adminstration
  (https://www.sba.gov/about-sba/sba-initiatives/small-business-Saturday)
- American Express
  (https://www.americanexpress.com/us/small-business/shop-small/)
- Facebook (https://www.facebook.com/SmallBusinessSaturday/)

### Phrases that Inspire Gift Purchases:

- Give the gift of health
- Your one-stop shop for gifts they'll love
- Gifts they will love—and are good for them!
- Our wellness products are one-size-fits-all gifts
- Massage makes everyone happy!
- Give yourself and others the gift of AHHHHHH this holiday!

## Closing the Sale

For some practitioners, selling products is as natural as booking the next session. Others struggle with both.

If you have done a thorough intake interview and truly listened to your clients, you have a fairly accurate knowledge of their needs and wants. After the one-on-one segment of the session is finished and the client is dressed, give a very brief overview of what took place in the session, highlight some of the client's major goals, assign homework, give the client an opportunity to ask questions, make any necessary referrals, discuss which products might be helpful to purchase (and sell those products or provide samples), and schedule the next appointment.

## Buying Cues

Some of the clues that a client is ready to make a purchase is that the client asks for more information about a product or instructions on how to use it, agrees with what is recommended during the post-session interview, or picks up and examines the product or literature. This is a green light for you to ask for the sale.

## Upselling

The perfect time to introduce additional products is after a client has decided to buy something. Just be certain that you are keeping the client's goals and needs in mind. Don't be pushy or aggressive and be conservative in the number of suggestions.

Think about what other products complement what the client has already chosen.

For instance, if a client has chosen a hot pack to help with his tight back, you might encourage him to purchase a topical analgesic or a self-massage tool. You could say something like, "Using this self-massage tool can also help in reducing tension between sessions. You can use it before or after the heat pack. Would you like me to give you a quick demonstration?"

Reflect on the client's stated needs as well as their lifestyle to make suggestions of products that they might enjoy. This is particularly applicable for items that might not be for pain management, but for general relaxation or pampering.

Upselling also includes selling a larger size (or multiple sizes) of a consumable product. If you carry different sizes of the same item, you can mention the cost benefits of the larger size and the convenience of the smaller size (particularly if it meets the TSA standards for airplane carryon items).

Package pricing is another popular upselling technique. Here are some examples:

- Offer a discount for purchasing several items in a line. For instance, give a discount when a client purchases a scrub, lotion, and body butter.
- Offer a "Buy 2 get the third at half price" when a client purchases 3 of the same item.
- Bundle products and give a discount.

## Wrapping It Up

Presentation is paramount! Whenever possible, avoid putting a client's purchases in a plain bag. Even a small purchase seems more special if it's packaged nicely. And who doesn't like a present—even when it's for themselves? In the very least, you should consider having season-

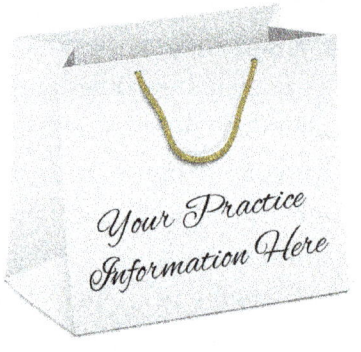

themed bags available for the holidays as people are likely to buy your products as gifts and you save them the time and expense of having to wrap it.

You can buy bags preprinted with your logo and company information or buy nice bags and affix labels onto them. Consider lining the bag and separating the items with colored tissue paper. Tie the tissue paper (or the bag itself if it has handles) with ribbon.

If you usually sell multiple items to a client at once, consider purchasing reusable cloth bags that have your logo, company name, website, and phone number printed on the outside. This option serves many purposes: it demonstrates your commitment to environmental responsibility; it's attractive; it conveys that you feel the products you sell are important; it becomes a marketing tool

in that the client is reminded of you every time that bag is used --
and if it's used in public (e.g., for groceries), other people see your
company information.

**Links to Bags and Boxes:**

- Bags and Bows (http://www.bagsandbows.com/)
- Howard Packaging (http://www.howardpkg.com/)
- Action Bag Company (http://www.actionbag.com/)

**Links to Promotional Printing Companies:**

- 4imprint (https://www.4imprint.com/)
- Amsterdam (http://www.amsterdamprinting.com/)
- Think Ink (http://www.wethinkpromos.com/)

# Fostering Ongoing Sales

If you're going to sell products at all, the key to working smarter—
not harder is to develop long-term product sales relationships with
your clients. Follow up on product sales, especially after the initial
sale. Contact clients several days after their session. Ask them how
they are enjoying the product, what results they notice, and what
questions they might have. If you gave them samples, ask if they
would like you to reserve or order a larger size. Consider sending a
thank-you note after the first sale or a large sale. Some practitioners
offer a modified type of frequent buyer plan that rewards clients
for their purchases. It could be a free product, a free service or a
special discount.

Make notes in your client files about their purchases and product
preferences. Review those files for important dates that could
lead to future purchases (e.g., birthdays, anniversaries, seasonal
changes, vacations).

The next time a client comes in after having made a purchase
during their last appointment, ask the following questions as part

of your session intake interview: how they liked the product, how effective was it (if applicable), how often they used it, and if they have any questions or concerns about the product.

Take the time to design a plan of action that fosters ongoing sales and notify current and potential clients of your products through newsletters, print materials, your website, and office signage.

## E-Commerce

Launching an online store is a good option—even for sole practitioners. The benefits are many, including increasing revenues and expanding market reach. An online store allows your current clients to get detailed information about your products at their leisure and helps you reach new customers both locally and outside of your local area.

According to the Nielsen Global Survey of E-Commerce (http:// www.nielsen.com/us/en/press-room/2014/global-online-purchase-intentions-have-doubled-since-2011-for-ebooks-toys-sporting-goods.html), approximately 60 percent of respondents stated that they browse products online before purchasing them in stores. Take advantage of this trend to increase the purchases that your clients make while at your office.

Technology has eased the process of creating an online store. The two major categories of e-commerce platforms are hosted and self-hosted.

As self-hosting implies, you do almost all of the work of building a website and an online store. This is not for the faint of heart. The advantage is that you have complete control over the site's content, appearance and function.

Most practitioners opt for a hosted version since those companies have dedicated support and their sites are usually stable. They provide a customizable online storefront, a secure shopping cart, and extensive support. These platforms support a variety of merchant payment services. Some also offer a low credit card processing fee if you use their merchant system; this option usually saves you the annual fee associated with getting your own Payment Card Industry (PCI) certification of compliance.

Generate traffic to your online store with your website, social media pages, and direct client communications (e.g., newsletters and email blasts). You can also place ads on Facebook and Google.

# 6
# Merchandising

Dictionary.com defines merchandising as: the planning and promotion of sales by presenting a product to the right market at the proper time, by carrying out organized, skillful advertising, using attractive displays, etc.

This chapter explores how to display products in a manner that draws clients'attention and inspires them to buy. Humans are sensitive; appeal to all the senses of sight, smell, hearing, touch, taste. The more you can do this, the easier it is for the products to essentially sell themselves.

## Visibility

Make sure people easily see what you have to sell. Don't place products behind a receptionist's desk where they might be unnoticed or inaccessible to clients. Display retail products throughout your office space in addition to a specific area that is dedicated to displaying your merchandise. Consider displaying retail sizes of certain products (e.g., the lotion you use in the session) in your treatment room.

Regardless of the size of your office, make your retail area attractive. Keep the space organized, clean, well lit, and appealing to all of the senses. Regularly wipe down all testers, remove dust bunnies or rancid product, and make sure labels, prices, and instructions are easy to read. If you don't have a waiting room, display products on a mirror or small glass shelf inside the session room, or on top of a rolling case if you do on-site work.

**Links to Product Cases:**

- Custom Case Company
  (http://www.customcasecompany.com/index.html)
- Bel-Air Shipping and Carrying Cases
  (http://www.bel-air-cases.com/)
- Fieldtex Cases (http://www.fieldtexcases.com/)
- Calibex (http://www.calibex.com/rolling-sales-case/shop-html)

Identify all products with price tags or signs. People might assume that the product is too expensive and not even ask. Also, utilize shelf talkers (signs or clips that draw attention to a product) to engage interest and boost sales.

**Eye Appeal = Buy Appeal**
**Eye Level = Buy Level**

## Design

Display your products in an eye-catching manner. In general, it's best to avoid just putting items on a shelf as they can easily get disorganized. Point-of-sale (POS) displays (also known as point-of purchase or POP) are effective ways to attractively display products. Get POS displays that fit easily onto a countertop, on a shelf, in a front room, or even on a table in the classroom. If you are unable to purchase POS units that are specifically designed for the products lines you carry, you can purchase them from companies that make generic units. Some of those companies can even customize your display unit.

## Links to Generic POS Display Units:

- Cardboard Displays (http://www.cardboarddisplays.com/)
- Displays 2 Go (http://www.displays2go.com/)

You can also put products in baskets or other containers. In one of my retailing workshops the participants had to design a marketing and merchandising plan for a specific product. The group that had the winning display idea were given foot products. They displayed an arrangement of foot balms, foot rollers, and other foot care products in a shoe. This could also be done to highlight a foot care bundle.

Arrange seating areas around product testing stations (e.g., essential oils, skin care products, self-care tools), and create a feature area to highlight new products and seasonal items. This feature area can be a separate section of the waiting area or an area created by using decorative items, rolled towels, baskets, or plants.

Consider putting a pitcher of water (perhaps with lemon slices) and glasses in the same area as your retail products. This way when clients walk over to get a drink, they see your products. When you encourage clients to arrive a few minutes before your session to update any paperwork and transition from the rest of their day to getting a session, it's likely that they will check out your products while waiting. The same is true for encouraging them to spend some time in the waiting room after a session before transitioning back into the world.

Display smaller impulse items, sale products, or new items on the front desk area. Change the general retail displays at least three times per year, placing new or seasonal items in featured areas. Change the items in the feature areas every four to eight weeks. Keep the display clean and dust-free; nothing discourages sales more than products that appear to be neglected on a counter.

Some other specific ways to be creative with your merchandising is to have themes for holidays and special events. You might put up signs or decorations or even carry special "seasonal" items.

For instance, at the holidays you could sell products that evoke the smell of pumpkin pie. Jenny Hogan, media director for Marketing Solutions Inc., suggests, "Use holiday decorations as a backdrop for retail sales. You can put gift certificates or holiday coupons in transparent ornaments and hang them on wreaths, garlands, or a Christmas tree." [vi]

## Impulse Buying

Impulse buying makes for a significant amount of sales. Think about the last time you went shopping. You had your list in hand and were ready to get what you needed. But then you pass by a display with an item that catches your eye. Perhaps it was a new item, was made from things you really like, or was on sale. The next thing you know, you are putting it into your cart. This item wasn't on your list, but it piqued your interest, reminded you that you were about to run low on a similar item, or inspired you to purchase it as a gift.

Smart marketers strategically place impulse items in areas where consumers are likely to pick them up. Grocery stores place items, such as candy, gum, and magazines in the checkout lane. Practitioners can follow that cue with healthy impulse items (e.g., essential oils, lip balms, CDs, DVDs, candles, jewelry).

An acupuncturist in Tucson has the following items on her checkout counter: a bowl with dried goji berries (and a spoon) for people to sample--right next to a couple of full bags of the berries; a display with organic beef jerky; packages of ginger candy, a box of individual packets of an electrolyte drink; tins of organic herbal throat mints; and a gift certificate with a bow. She has her other retail products (herbs, supplements, liniments, and miscellaneous self-care items) on a nearby display case.

## Holiday Merchandising

Set a festive tone by decorating your office. Include a variety of holiday motifs (e.g., Merry Christmas, Happy Hanukkah, Joyous Kwanzaa, and the broad category of Seasons Greetings). Here are some fun ideas for creating an inviting holiday ambiance: hang posters and signs; apply rub-on window decorations; string colorful lights; arrange holiday plants (e.g., holly, poinsettias, Christmas cactus); use sheets that have holiday prints or colors; serve hot cider and healthy treats; gently diffuse seasonal scents such as pine, frankincense, and vanilla; and play a variety of holiday music.

Attractively present your holiday gift packages. A simple gift box, organza bag, or even a ribbon can easily do the trick. A fun Hanukkah idea is to dress up the packages with a mesh bag tied with a light blue ribbon that contains a miniature dreidel and chocolate gelt. You can attach a candy cane or even mistletoe to packages for a Christmas theme. Kwanzaa candle colors are green, red, and black; get one of each, tie them with a colorful piece of material, and attach it to one of your product displays. When you have product bundles that are already "pre-wrapped" you save your clients even more time—and that alone can increase your holiday sales. Stock wrapping supplies and offer to supply them for clients who purchase other items for gifts.

Put your holiday items on a focus area in your waiting room or a tray in your office. One of my clients put up a Christmas tree and placed several presents (of differing prices) under the tree that her clients could see. She had additional stock behind the counter ready for purchase. You could even attach a gift certificate to a "holiday" plant or decoration.

You can have a lot of fun and express your creativity through artsy projects such as creating a diorama with the theme "Joys of the Season" that displays various products as part of the story.

## On-Site Merchandising Tips

For those of you who do mostly on-site work, you can still create a holiday environment. Assemble a kit of items in a small box. The box becomes the stand. Drape a piece of colorful material over the box and display your items (e.g., candles, a small silk plant). An effective visual way to inform your on-site clients about your holiday specials is to take pictures of your holiday packages and make a small poster (with a heading such as "Healthy Holiday Gift Ideas"), attach the print to a cardboard picture frame, and unobtrusively place the frame on your display box.

# Epilogue

We hope that after reading this book you are inspired to elevate the way you sell products in your practice. This could range from being willing to even consider adding retailing to your practice, to expanding the products you carry, to improving the methods you use to sell products.

We wish you good fortune and safe travels on your retailing journey! Please refer to the following tips for inspiration.

## Retail Mastery Tips

### Tips for Choosing Products

- Conduct product research before you offer products for resell.
- Try a product before offering it in any session or for retail in your practice.
- Educate yourself and your staff on the products you use and sell.
- Sell only products that fit into the type of work you do or gift items that align with your image.
- Choose products you trust and believe in.
- Ask clients what products they would like you to carry.
- Find products that aren't easily accessible to your clients.
- Consider creating a private-label product to foster customer loyalty and boost retail sales.
- Properly assess clients' needs and match up appropriate products.
- Educate clients on the proper use of products.
- Inspire clients to use the products at home by suggesting how and when to do that.
- Purchase products from a distributor or manufacturer that

offers marketing support.

- Offer samples to your clients. If a client tries and likes a product, the product will sell itself!

## Tips for Managing Finances

- Charge a fair but profitable price.
- Keep track of your sales and inventory.
- Know your local, state, and federal tax laws.

## Tips for Selling Products

- During the post-interview, encourage questions about the products used during the session.
- Ask clients for their reaction to, and opinions on, the products being sold.
- Make recommendations for homework and products during the post-interview.
- Selling isn't Telling. Selling is first, and foremost, about listening.
- Offer Signature Treatments and special holiday treatments to increase your product sales.
- Include products whenever you host open houses or give public presentations.
- Host product education and sampling events.
- Start a product review club.
- When clients purchase a consumable product, flag their files for the recommended date of repurchase and send them a reminder.
- Bundle items.
- Utilize products (that you also sell) during the session.
- Print flyers that describe all the products you carry.
- Promote product specials in your waiting area, newsletters, social media, and website.

- Make price sheets and recommendation sheets available for clients.
- Pay attention to client buying cues.
- Whenever possible, put the client's purchases in an attractive bag.
- The perfect time to introduce additional products is after a client has decided to buy something.
- Plan well in advance for holiday promotions.

## Tips for Merchandising

- Display your products and promotional literature in your waiting area.
- Make the products visible and attractive.
- Put the products on display so clients can see, feel, and smell the products.
- Bring a carrying case that serves as a mini shelving unit to display products for on-site treatments.
- Put price stickers on your products.
- Utilize Shelf Talkers.
- Put testers on display.
- Strategically place impulse items in areas where clients are likely to pick them up.
- Keep the display area clean, organized, and well lit.
- Choose a limited number of products to spotlight on a monthly basis.
- If you carry self-health DVDs, play them before and after sessions in the waiting area.

# Endnotes

[i]   Marshall Dahneke and Lynda Solien-Wolfe. "Passion, Products & Profit: A Way to Boost Your Business" Massage Today April 2017, Vol 17, Issue 04

[ii]  Bridgette Redman and Elizabeth Johnson, Retail Management for Spas. (ISPA Foundation and American Hotel and Lodging Educational Institute, 2005), 10.

[iii] Michel Tuan Pham, Iris Hung, and Gerald Gorn. "Relaxation Increases Monetary Valuations." Journal of Marketing Research 48, no. 5 (October 2011): 814-826. P 6

[iv]  From a survey of massage therapists commissioned by MASSAGE Magazine and conducted by Lewis & Clark survey company in 2013.

[v]   Anita Shannon. "How can offering retail products benefit my clients and help me to be recognized as a health care specialist?" MASSAGE Magazine August 2011 pp 22

[vi]  Phyllis Hanton, "Holiday Spa Treatments: A Festive Touch," MASSAGE Magazine December 2014  22-25

CPSIA information can be obtained
at www.ICGtesting.com
Printed in the USA
LVHW02s0145010218
564679LV00001B/1/P